THESE JOKES ARE SO SICK . . .

What are a Mexican cannibal's favorite leftovers?

Refried beings.

What did the sign in the window of the gay bar say?

NO CHICKS ACCEPTED

How do you tell the difference between a Jew and an Italian?

The Jew's the one in the Italian suit.

THEY'RE *UTTERLY GROSS!*

FAVORITE GROSS SELECTIONS
by Julius Alvin

GROSS LIMERICKS (1375, $2.50)

This masterpiece collection offers the funniest of rhythmical rhymes, from all your favorite categories of humor. And they're true-to-form, honest-to-goodness, GROSS LIMERICKS!

GROSS GIFTS (1111, $2.50)

It's the Encyclopedia Grossitanica, with everything from gross books to gross cosmetics, and from gross movies to gross vacations. It's all here in the thoroughly and completely tasteless and tacky atalogue we call . . . GROSS GIFTS!

OSS JOKES (1244, $2.50)

haven't read it all—until you read GROSS JOKES! This lete compilation is guaranteed to deliver the sickest, sassiest !

LY GROSS JOKES (1333, $2.50)

tasteless ridiculous to the taboo sublime, TOTALLY OKES has enough laughs in store for even *the most* humor fanatics.

erever paperbacks are sold, or order direct from the nd cover price plus 50¢ per copy for mailing and bra Books, 475 Park Avenue South, New York, N.Y. T SEND CASH.

Utterly GROSS JOKES

By Julius Alvin

ZEBRA BOOKS
KENSINGTON PUBLISHING CORP.

ZEBRA BOOKS

are published by

Kensington Publishing Corp.
475 Park Avenue South
New York, N.Y. 10016

SECOND PRINTING FEBRUARY 1984

Printed in the United States of America

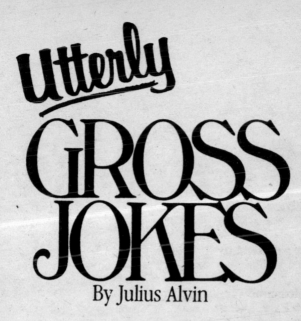

Utterly GROSS JOKES

By Julius Alvin

CONTENTS

Chapter One

UTTERLY REVOLTING RACIAL AND ETHNIC JOKES

Why did it take the Polish couple a week to drive from New York to Boston?

They kept seeing signs in service stations that said, "Clean Rest Rooms."

Why was the wheelbarrow invented in Africa?

So blacks could learn to walk on their hind legs.

Why was the black woman mad at her husband?

Because he was off shooting craps and she didn't know how to cook them.

Did you hear about the Jewish terrorists who hijacked a plane?

They demanded ten million dollars in pledges.

Did you hear about the black man who suffered from insomnia?

He kept waking up every few days.

Why couldn't the Polack count to ten?

One of his fingers was missing.

What's Poland's solution to the oil crisis?

Import a million tons of Arabian sand and dig their own wells.

Why aren't there any dogs in the Vatican?

Because they pee on poles.

Why was the Polack so happy?

He found out he could play his AM radio in the afternoon.

A WASP husband was humping his wife when suddenly, to his intense surprise, she wiggled and let out with a short cry of delight.

"My God, honey!" he exclaimed. "What happened?"

"It's wonderful," she said. "I finally decided that those curtains would look much better in peach."

What's the definition of a macho WASP?

One who jogs home from his vasectomy.

Did you hear about the WASP woman who decided to eat caviar instead of taking birth control pills?

She heard it was inconceivably delicious.

How can you tell a WASP widow?

She's the one in black tennis clothes.

How did the Polish mother finally stop her kid from biting nails?

She made him wear shoes.

Why did the Polish Army form an attack force consisting solely of epileptics?

So the enemy couldn't tell which ones had been shot.

What does a bride at a Southern wedding do immediately after the preacher pronounces the couple man and wife?

Tells her father to lower the shotgun.

What's the first thing a Russian woman has to do before she takes a bath?

Grease the sides of the tub so she doesn't stick.

How do you break a Polack's finger?

Punch him in the nose.

An Italian girl fell in love with a classical musician, but her mother was violently opposed to the match.

"What's wrong?" the musician asked. "I make a good living."

"My mother thinks you're too feminine," the girl said.

"She may have a point," the musician said. "Her mustache is a lot thicker than mine."

What do they call the brother of an Italian mother?

A monkey's uncle.

What do you call an Italian woman?

A pizza ass.

How can you sink an Argentine submarine?

Put it in the water.

How can you spot an Argentinian tank?

It has back-up lights.

Why did the British government get such a good price for the Argentine weapons they captured?

None of them had been fired more than once.

Why did most Argentine planes fail to reach the Falkland Islands?

The rubberbands broke.

What's the first clothing item issued an Argentine Army recruit?

A white handkerchief.

What's the thinnest book in the world?

ARGENTINE WAR HEROES

Why did the Italian salesman quit his new job?

The boss gave him a virgin territory.

Why did the Polack spend three hours in the car wash?

It was raining too hard to drive.

Two blacks were driving down a Southern road when they spotted a stray pig. Unable to resist, they loaded the pig into the car and took off.

They were going so fast that a white cop pulled them over for speeding. While the officer approached the car, the two men hurriedly covered the pig with a sheet.

"What are you two doing?" the officer asked.

"Why, we were just lookin' for women," one black replied.

At that point, the pig stuck its head out from under the sheet and looked at the cop.

The cop shook his head sadly, then said to the pig, "What's a nice Southern girl like you doing in a car with two niggers?"

How does a WASP couple define sexual compatability?

Both of them have headaches every night at ten.

What do the Post Office and the Kinney Shoe Company have in common?

500,000 loafers.

Why don't more black women become nuns?

Because they can't remember to say "Superior" after "Mother."

What's the definition of a black genius?

A man who can name his own children.

"My wife is a typical WASP," the man complained to his companion on the commuter train to Connecticut. "She'll only make love doggie style."

"Doggie style? I don't believe it," the companion said.

"Yeah. I sit up and beg, then she rolls over and plays dead."

Where's the safest place to hide money from your black housekeeper?

Under the soap.

What's a black virgin?

An ugly first grader.

How can you tell a Polish woman is having her period?

When she's only wearing one sock.

What's the most profitable use of an extra closet?

Rent it to a Vietnamese family.

A black guy walked into a travel agency looking for adventure. The agent told him about a great deal—a day drifting down a river, then a champagne party at the end. The cost was only $200.

The black guy paid his money, and boarded a bus. But when he got to the river, he was grabbed by two huge guys, strapped naked to a log, and chucked into the water. He sped downstream, battered by rocks, nearly drowned by spray. Finally, he got a break when his log spun into a little inlet near shore.

When he got his breath, the black guy noticed a Polack tied to a log floating next to him. "Hey," the black guy called, "do we get champagne at the end of this trip?"

"We didn't last year," the Polack replied.

What's the most sought-after rank in the Greek Navy?

Rear Admiral.

One day a Ku Klux Klan member felt like pursuing his favorite sport—driving around the country looking for blacks to run over with his pickup truck. After about a half-hour, he saw a black figure up ahead and he tromped on the gas. But as he got closer, he saw the black figure was really a priest carrying an empty gas can.

The Klan member pulled over and offered the priest a ride to the gas station. Sure enough, on the way back to the priest's car, there was a veritable stream of blacks walking by the road. The Klan member had trouble keeping himself under control. But when he saw a big hulking black with a sassy look on his face, he couldn't resist.

He pretended to fall asleep at the wheel and let the car drift over to the side of the road. Then he heard a loud "BANG."

The Klan member slammed on his brakes and said to the priest, "Father, did I hit him?"

"No," the priest replied. "But you got close enough for me to whack him with my gas can."

Is it true Mexicans catch fish without hooks or nets?

It's true. They just lower their ass in the water, fart, and the fish jump on shore.

How did the Polish entrepreneur become a millionaire?

He took a plane to America, bought up 100,000 metal coat hangers, took them back to Poland, and sold them as home abortion kits.

What's the definition of frenzy?

An Italian with a credit card in a whorehouse.

Why can't you ever hire two Greek men in the same department?

Because they'll always find a way to get a little behind in their work.

Why does it take four Polacks to pop corn?

One to hold the pan, and three to shake the stove.

An enlightened Southern boy brought a black friend home from college one weekend. His parents were very wealthy, and they lived on a huge estate on an island about a mile off the coast of Georgia. To celebrate their son's visit, the parents threw a big party on their huge dock, right on the water.

Near the end of the party, the father, who'd put back a lot of bourbon, yelled for everybody's attention. He announced that the mile-long stretch of water between the island and the mainland was infested with man-eating sharks. Anybody who dared swim that stretch and survived, he offered, could have the choice of his house, his business, or his beautiful young daughter.

A moment later, there was a splash, and the black college student was swimming like a whirlwind. The father and the son jumped in their motor boat, but the black guy beat them to the mainland.

"Well," the father said. "I'm a man of my word. You can have my house, my business, or my daughter."

"I don't want any of them," the black man said angrily, "I just want that mutherfucker who pushed me in."

Two Polacks walked into a bar. The bartender asked them, "What has four legs and stinks?"

"I don't know," one replied.

"You and your friend," the bartender said.

Later, the two Polacks were walking down the street when they spotted two men. One Polack said to them, "What has four legs and stinks?"

The two men said they didn't know.

"Me and my friend," the Polack replied.

The black dude came home unexpectedly early one day to find his wife lying in bed, naked and exhausted. The sheets were all rumpled, and a damp towel was on the bed.

"What you been doin'?" the dude asked.

"I'm feeling poorly," she replied. "I couldn't get out of bed all day."

"And what about the towel?"

"I dampened it to put on my head."

The black dude went into the bathroom and came back with a long, gleaming straight razor.

"What's that for?" his wife asked anxiously.

"If that towel dries soft," the dude said, "I'm gonna shave."

What's the definition of a redneck?

A guy who'll screw a black girl, but won't go to school with her.

Why is a tampon like a Jewish American Princess?

Because they're both stuck up cunts.

What does a football and a Polish girl have in common?

Pigskin.

What's the most dangerous event in a Polish track and field meet?

Catching the javelin.

What's a Polish martini?

An olive in a glass of beer.

How do Italian girls protect themselves from peeping toms?

They keep the curtains open.

What's the definition of an erection on a Polack?

A ski lift.

Did you hear about the desperate young Polish girl?

She sent change-of-address cards to peeping toms.

"I'm sure my Leroy's foolin' around these days," the black woman said to her friend.

"How kin you tell?"

"The last couple childs we had don't look nothin' like him."

What's the Arab battle flag?

A white handkerchief.

How do you tell the difference between a Jew and an Italian?

The Jew is the one in the Italian suit.

Two Jewish men were talking. One said to the other, "Did you hear what Rosenberg did to his girl friend?"

"No."

"Well, she's been leading him on for six months. Finally, he nailed her tits together."

"My God," the friend said. "Why?"

"Rosenberg's philosophy is, if you can't lick 'em, join 'em."

Mrs. Goldberg walked into a butcher shop and asked the owner for a fresh chicken. When he brought one out, she lifted the wing and smelled it. "Ugh!" she exclaimed. "It smells."

Then she pulled up a leg and repeated, "Ugh!"

Finally, she smelled the hind end. After holding her nose, she told the butcher, "How could you call this a fresh chicken?"

"Mrs. Goldberg," he calmly replied. "Tell me. Could you survive such an inspection?"

Did you hear about the ugly Polish baby?

For the first six months, they diapered the wrong end.

What do they call the Polish edition of WHO'S WHO?

WHAT'S THAT?

How did the Mexican woman take off 20 pounds in one day?

She washed off her makeup.

Why don't Italian women shave their legs?

They just put them up in curlers.

Why couldn't the Italian man buy his wife a mink coat?

The fur clashed with her moustache.

What's the most effective birth control device for an Italian woman?

Her face.

How fat are Russian women?

They have to bat their eyelashes by hand.

Why do Jewish women make such good tuba players?

Their mouths are so big they can play the tuba from either end.

What's the best-selling brand of tooth cleaner in Poland?

Sandpaper.

Why did God give Italians arms?

So their fingers wouldn't smell like their armpits.

Why do Arab women wear veils?

So they can blow their nose without getting their hands dirty.

How do Eskimos give birth?

They rub noses and the little buggers fall out.

Why is the camel called the "ship of the desert?"

Because it's filled with Arab semen.

Why did the Polack cross the road?

To get to the middle.

What color is a Negro who's been run over by a steam roller?

Flat black.

What does NAACP stand for?

Niggers Are Actually Colored Polacks.

What's the difference between garbage and an Irish girl?

Garbage gets picked up.

What's the definition of a nigger?

A Negro who just left the room.

What do you do when an Arab throws a pin at you?

Run like hell. He's probably holding a grenade in his mouth.

How do you tell a WASP family at a Chinese restaurant?

They're the ones sitting at the table where nobody's sharing.

A Jewish American Princess was shopping at Bloomingdale's. She walked over to the perfume to inspect the merchandise. She picked up a quarter-ounce bottle worth $500, opened the top to take a sniff, then dropped the bottle, spilling the entire contents on the rug.

A distraught salesperson rushed over. "Don't worry," the JAP assured her. "I'm not hurt at all."

How many Polacks does it take to hang a picture?

Five. One to hold the hammer and four to push the wall.

Why couldn't the Polack be buried at sea?

Because the funeral director died trying to dig his grave.

Why do Mexicans eat beans for dinner?

So they can take bubble baths later.

How do Arabs make shish kebob?

They shoot an arrow into a rotting camel.

Why do haircuts cost $25 in Poland?

Because it's so hard to cut around the corners.

How do they make Italian sausage?

From retarded pigs.

Why do blacks put doormats inside the house?

So they don't get the streets dirty when they go out.

Why don't blacks ever drown?

Their lips are built-in inner tubes.

The young man walked into the New York City employment office to apply for a job as a lifeguard. The Jewish clerk said, "All you have to do is answer one question: Do you know how to save Puerto Ricans from drowning?"

Stunned, the young man replied, "Uh, no."

"Good," the clerk said. "You're hired."

Why hasn't a Polish driver ever won the Indianapolis 500?

Because they have to keep stopping to ask for directions.

What's a Mexican car pool?

Five Mexicans pushing a car to the unemployment office.

What's the definition of a black loser?

One who doesn't have carfare to get down to apply for welfare.

Why didn't the Spanish Armada conquer England?

The oil slick gave them away.

What do products manufactured in Puerto Rico have imprinted on them?

"Untouched by human hands."

What do they call girls' dorms at Polish universities?

Pig stys.

Why did the aquarium in Warsaw close down?

The clams all died.

What's the difference between an Irish wedding and an Irish funeral?

One less drunk.

What do they call a stork that delivers babies in Harlem?

A dope peddler.

What's the most common Polish wedding proposal?

"You're gonna have a what?"

What do virgin Polish brides wear at their wedding?

White overalls.

How do Polacks reproduce?

They exchange underwear.

Why did the birth rate in Russia go up so drastically?

The waiting list to have an abortion got to be ten months long.

Why did the wealthy fisherman marry a Mexican woman?

Because she had a fine crop of worms.

How do you brainwash an Italian?

Step on his enema bag.

Why do Mexicans save the pull rings off beer cans?

To use as class rings.

Why do Italians save the pull rings off beer cans?

To use as nose pickers.

How do we know Batman is Polish?

He wears his jockey shorts over his leotards.

How was streaking invented?

They tried to give a black dude a bath.

Why do we know that Adam was Polish?

Who else would have stood beside a naked woman and just munched on an apple?

Why don't Puerto Ricans take the skin off bananas before they eat them?

Because they know what's inside.

Why don't people in Poland believe in reincarnation?

Who wants to die and come back a Polack?

Why aren't there any salt shakers in Polish households?

Because the housewives find it too hard to get the salt in through those little holes.

What's the one advantage to being Polish?

You never miss an important call because you're in the bathtub.

Do all Polish teachers have ESP?

Yes. Extra Simple Pupils.

How can you tell a Polish pencil?

It has an eraser at both ends.

Chapter Two

UTTERLY APPALLING ANIMAL JOKES

A man joined the French Foreign Legion and reported to a post way out in the desert. After a few lonely days, he asked his sergeant, "What do you do for women around here?"

"Once a month," the sergeant replied, "a pack of camels comes into camp."

"Yuch," the recruit said, walking away before the sergeant could say more. After another couple of weeks, though, he was horny as hell when the camels came into the camp. Before they could even be tethered, he grabbed one, mounted it, and shot his wad.

"What do you think you're doing?" the sergeant screamed. "You're supposed to ride the camel to a whorehouse in town."

A Greek who had moved to Athens and become rich took his wife back to his native village to show her around. They were walking in the fields when the Greek said to the woman, "It's over there, my darling, under that tree, that I had my first sex."

"Did anyone find out?" the wife asked.

"Her mother was watching at the time," the Greek said.

His wife was shocked. "What did she say?"

"Baaaaa."

A very rich woman had a parrot who could talk and sing in four languages. The parrot was a huge hit at parties, and the woman adored him. But he had one weakness: he kept escaping out to the hen house to fuck the chickens.

The woman tried everything to cure the parrot of the habit. Finally, she got scissors and clipped all the feathers off the parrot's head. "That should teach you," she said.

Two nights later she had a party. The parrot was in its usual spot on the piano as the guests came in. Halfway through the party, two bald men arrived.

"Hey," the parrot called out, "will you two chicken fuckers get over here?"

The ventriloquist was driving through the country when he got a flat tire. He didn't have a spare tire, so he hitched a ride to a farm.

The farmer was working on his tractor, so the ventriloquist had to wait. To amuse himself, he began to practice his craft. He made one of the horses talk.

The farmer was amazed. He called his wife, his daughter, and his son. When they arrived, a rooster greeted them.

The wife, farmer, and daughter were agape. But the son turned white. He turned to his father and said, "If that little sheep says anything about me, it's a damn lie!"

A farmer was charged with having intercourse with a calf. The judge said, "Harry, this is a serious thing. How could you?"

"Well," the farmer said, "my wife died a year ago, and I've been feeling mighty lonely. I finally couldn't resist one day. I put a milking stool behind the calf and mounted her. But you know what, Judge? That calf pissed all over me."

The judge grimaced. "I know. Those calves do that every time."

What's a fly's favorite fast food?

Kentucky Fried Chickenshit

The druggist couldn't help noticing a man who came in every week to buy two dozen rubbers. Finally, his curiosity got the best of him, and he said, "You must have the stamina of a bull. How do you get it up so often?"

"I beg your pardon," the man said prissily. "I find the whole idea of sex repulsive."

"Then why do you use so many rubbers?"

"I taught my poodle to swallow them. Now she shits in little plastic bags."

Why did the veterinarian's wife divorce him?

For fooling around with a female patient.

Did you hear about the shepherd who was into S & M?

He put a leather leash on his sheep before he fucked her.

"I had a problem with my dog," a man said to a friend. "No matter how often I walked him, he'd shit all over the floor every chance he'd get."

"Did you get rid of him?" the friend asked.

"No, the kids would have killed me. I spent $100 to send him to obedience school for training."

"Did that work?"

The guy grimaced. "He stopped shitting on the floor. But now he sits on the toilet for an hour smoking cigars and reading the funny pages."

What's the best-selling adult sex toy in Scotland?

Fur-covered inflatable sheep.

A shepherd came down from the pasture and went to see his doctor, who told him he had VD.

"I was afraid of that," the shepherd said.

The doctor gave him a shot of penicillin. Then the shepherd asked, "Do you treat animals?"

"Of course not," the doctor said. "I'm not a vet."

"Damn," the shepherd said. "If I've got VD, my flock has it, too."

The woman was seeing her doctor about a knee problem. They were all scratched and bleeding.

"How did this happen?" the doctor asked.

The woman blushed. Finally, she admitted, "To tell you the truth, I've been . . . been doing it doggie fashion."

"Well, that's easy enough to cure," the doctor said. "Just roll over and do it in the missionary position."

"I've tried it," the girl complained, "but every time I do, my dog's breath is so bad it knocks me out."

To see which of three suitors would get the hand of his beautiful daughter, the farmer said, "Whichever of you can screw that cow up on the hill the longest, gets to marry my daughter."

The first guy tried his best, but could only last 30 minutes. The second grunted and strained and managed to stay in an hour. But the third pumped away nearly half the night.

"All right, son," the farmer said, "my daughter is yours."

"To hell with your daughter," the man replied. "How much do you want for the cow?"

Early one Sunday morning, a veterinarian had a phone call from a little old lady who asked him how to separate two dogs that were mating on her front lawn. "Try using a broom handle," the vet said.

A few minutes later, the old lady called back again to report the dogs were still going at it. "Try tossing a bucket of water on them," the vet said.

But the phone rang again. The doctor curtly said, "Why don't you tell the male dog the phone is ringing for him."

"Do you think that will really work?" the old lady asked.

"Damn right," the vet grunted. "It's worked three times for me."

Why did the 3-legged dog walk into the bar?

He was looking for the scoundrel that shot his paw.

A group of scientists decided to conduct an experiment to see if the pets of people in various professions picked up any of their owners' habits. They rounded up a mathematician and his dog, an engineer and his dog, and an actor and his dog.

First, they placed the mathematician's dog in a room with a pile of bones and closed the door. When they returned a half-hour later, the dog had arranged the bones in an arithmatic progression: 1, 2, 3, 4, etc.

The engineer's dog was left alone for a half-hour. When the scientists came back, they found the dog had constructed a scale model of a drawbridge with the bones.

Excited to confirm their theory about dogs picking up habits, the scientists brought the actor's pet into the room. He immediately ate all the bones, fucked the two other dogs, then demanded to go home early.

Chapter Three

UTTERLY MORTIFYING MEDICAL JOKES

A girl went to a doctor and complained, "I've been having trouble lately. Every time I get even the tiniest cut, it takes forever to stop bleeding."

"That's interesting," the doctor replied. "How much do you lose when you get your period?"

"About $2000 that week," she replied.

A Chinaman went to a doctor because he was constipated. The doctor prescribed a laxative, and told him to come back in three days.

The Chinaman dutifully reported back. The doctor asked, "Did you move?"

The Chinaman replied, "No movee. Me no movee."

The doctor doubled the prescription. Three days later the Chinaman came back, and in response to the doctor's question again replied, "No movee. Me no movee."

The doctor doubled the strength of the laxative again. Three days later he came back and the doctor asked, "Did you move?"

The Chinaman replied, "Yes, me movee this morning. House full of shit."

Why is a gynecologist like an incurable gossip?

He spends a lot of time spreading old wives' tails.

What do people with incurable bad breath do?

Become dentists.

A young Russian girl was being examined by a gynecologist. He asked her to spread her legs, then winced at the horrible smell caused by a couple of infections.

"God!" the doctor exclaimed, "it looks like you've never had a check up there."

"I have too," the girl said indignantly. "And a few Hungarians and Yugoslavs, besides!"

A young man from a small Southern town was subpoenaed to take a blood test to see if he was the father of a teenage girl's baby. He was scared to death before he took the test, but after he came out of the hospital, he was smiling and confident.

"Did the test show you were the father?" one of his friends asked.

"No way," the Southerner said. "Stupid doctor took the samples from my finger!"

Why did the doctor give the lady golfer ten suppositories?

That was par for her hole.

A woman went to a psychiatrist and complained, "Doctor, my husband thinks he's a magician."

"What's so bad about that?" the shrink asked.

"We're being sued. A week ago my husband shoved a girl into a trunk and sawed it in half."

"The girl's family is suing you?" the psychiatrist asked.

"No, the circus," the woman replied. "The elephant bled to death."

What's a psychiatrist?

A doctor who can't stand the sight of blood.

What's the only way a Polish girl could get an appointment with a plastic surgeon?

A blind date.

How do proctologists examine their patients?

Rear view mirrors.

Why did Dolly Parton's teeth fall out?

Her dentist couldn't reach them.

How did the nurse punish her demanding patient?

She dipped her rectal thermometers in Ben-Gay.

A patient scheduled to undergo mouth surgery confided his most horrible fears to a nurse.

"Will I die? Will I be disfigured? I don't know what's going to happen."

"Don't worry," the pretty nurse said. "Your surgeon is a specialist and you'll receive the best of care."

"You're right," the patient said. "I'll probably laugh about oral surgery in the morning."

"Laugh?" the nurse scoffed. "With no lips?"

What's a dermatologist's favorite entertainment?

Skin flicks.

Chapter Four

UTTERLY INDECENT RELIGIOUS JOKES

Why didn't Jesus eat M & M's?

They kept falling through the holes in his hands.

Moses and Jesus were out fishing on a wide lake in heaven when they started talking about old times. "Are you still up to snuff?" Jesus asked.

"I don't know," Moses replied. He stood up, raised his hands, and suddenly the water parted. The boat dropped, coming to a jarring halt on dry sand. Then Moses lowered his hands and the water rushed back in.

"Not bad," Jesus said. "Let me try my trick." He jumped out of the boat and began walking to shore. But after a couple steps, he suddenly plunged beneath the waves.

Moses jumped in, pulled Jesus into the boat, then asked, "What happened?"

"I should have known," Jesus groused. "Last time I tried this, I didn't have holes in my feet."

The very naive young nun was assigned to a parish in the country. On the first Saturday, the priest asked her if she wanted to go swimming. She'd never been before, but the priest promised he'd give her lessons.

They changed into bathing suits, then the priest offered her a hand while they waded into the water. They splashed around for a few minutes until the nun turned to the priest and asked, "Father, will I really drown if you take your fingers out of my hole?"

The priest found himself incredibly attracted to a beautiful young woman who came to him confessing that she'd been unable to resist a man's advances. He put his arm around the girl's shoulder and asked, "Did the man do this, my dear?"

"Yes, Father."

The priest kissed her. "Did he do this?"

"Yes, and worse."

The priest lifted up her skirt and fingered her precious jewels. "Did he do this?"

"Yes, Father, and worse," the girl said.

The priest had lost control by this time. He threw the girl down to the floor and stuck his dick in her up to the hilt. "Did he do this?" the priest panted.

"Yes, Father, and worse."

"How could he do worse?" the priest demanded.

"He gave me gonorrhea," the girl said.

A married woman was in bed with a man when her husband came home unexpectedly. The man hopped out of bed and dashed into the closet. He was trembling already, but he nearly leaped out of his skin when he felt a tap on his knee.

"Hey, mister," said a small voice.

The man looked down and saw a little boy who'd been hiding in the closet. "Shhh," the man said.

"It's dark in here," the little boy said. "I want to get out."

"I'll give you ten dollars," the man whispered. The boy shook his head. "Twenty? Thirty?"

Finally, the boy decided he'd stay in the closet for $50. Later that day, the boy's father took him out shopping. The kid saw a bicycle and said he wanted it. "That costs $50," the father said. The boy showed him ten $5 bills.

The father was astounded, then demanded to know where the boy got the money. The boy wouldn't say, so the father drove him to church and demanded he go to confession and tell the priest how he came by the money.

The boy entered the confessional and closed the door. The priest slid back the panel and said, "Tell me your sins, my son."

The boy said, "I don't want to. It's dark in here."

"You're not starting that again," the priest said.

Sister Margaret died, and through some grievous error, wound up in hell instead of heaven. She got on the phone to Saint Peter to tell him a horrible mistake had been made. Saint Peter promised to get right on it.

The next day, however, the good sister was still with all the sinners. Saint Peter received a second panicked call. "This is Sister Margaret again. You've got to help me. There's an orgy scheduled for first thing tomorrow morning."

Saint Peter again promised to get right on it, but the next day he once again absentmindedly forgot. About noon he received another call. "Hey, Pete, this is Maggie. Forget about the transfer!"

What do you call big, ugly, hairy nuns who drive motorcycles?

Hell's Angels of Mercy.

What's black and white and has a dirty name?

Sister Mary Fuck-face.

A drunken man who reeked of whiskey, cigars, and cheap perfume staggered up the steps into the bus, reeled down the aisle, then plopped himself down on a seat next to a priest. The drunk took a long look at his rather offended seat partner, then said, "Hey, Father. I gotta question for you. What causes arthritis?"

The priest's reply was cold and curt. "Amoral living," he said. "Too much liquor, smoking, and consorting with loose women."

"Huh," the drunk said. "Well, I'll be damned."

They rode in silence for a moment. The priest began to feel guilty that he'd reacted so strongly to a man who obviously needed Christian compassion. He turned to the man and said, "I'm sorry, my son. I didn't mean to be harsh. How long have you suffered from your terrible affliction of arthritis?"

"My affliction?" the drunk said. "I don't have arthritis. I was just reading in the paper that the Pope had it."

Chapter Five

UTTERLY TASTY CANNIBAL AND VAMPIRE JOKES

What kind of party did the girlfriends of the female vampire give her before her wedding?

A blood bath.

What meal do cannibals make from politicians?

Bologna sandwiches.

What are Mexican cannibals' favorite leftovers?

Refried beings.

How do cannibals cook politicians?

In a crock pot.

Why would Ronald Reagan never be captured by cannibals?

He's too hard to swallow.

A tribe of cannibals was out hunting when they came across a hunter. They immediately captured him and tossed him in a pot for lunch. When he was done, they cut him up and passed out the parts.

One cannibal noticed that the cannibal who got the man's sexual organ, which was considered a delicacy, hadn't touched a bite. "What's the matter?" the one cannibal asked.

"I'm going to wait until we get back home where there's a soda machine," the second cannibal replied. "You know, things go better with Coke."

What do they dissect in vampire biology classes?

Frogmen.

What's a vampire's favorite popsicle?

Frozen used tampons.

What's a vampire's favorite kind of music?

Ragtime.

What's the most popular government job in Transylvania?

Kotex collector.

A vampire walked into a men's store and asked to see some men's shirts. When the salesgirl looked into his dark eyes, she was hypnotized. He fell on her, sunk his fangs, and took a drink. When he awakened her, she remembered nothing. He bought a shirt and left.

The next night, she was surprised to see the vampire back again. "Want to try something different tonight, sir?" the young lass asked.

"No," the vampire said with an evil grin. "Something in exactly the same vein."

How did Count Dracula die?

He bit a leukemia patient and got food poisoning.

Why did the crematorium export its ashes to Africa?

They sold them to cannibals as instant people.

Two African travelers were set upon by cannibals and overcome. They were carted back to camp, stripped, prodded and poked, then dumped in a pot of water over a raging fire. A couple of minutes later, two male cannibals came over to the pot and started to masturbate.

"This is the final indignity!" one traveler said.

"Shut up!" the cannibal chief ordered. "It's no insult. They're just adding the cream sauce."

Two cannibals captured an explorer and his lovely young bride. One cannibal immediately filled a pot with water, lit a fire, and tossed the explorer in.

"Come on," he said to his friend, "it's time to put your dinner in."

"Go ahead without me," the friend said, leering at the beautiful girl, "I think I'll eat mine raw."

What happened to the Italian woman who was captured by cannibals?

They threw her away and cooked her clothes.

Chapter Six

UTTERLY FOUL HOMOSEXUAL JOKES

How did the boy feel when he first discovered he was homosexual?

It was quite a blow.

Two college students had made love all night, then lay back in an embrace. After a few minutes, one turned to the other and said, "Bill, will you always love me the way you did tonight?"

"Yes, dear," he murmured.

"Will you love my soft lips, my big brown eyes, my soft skin?"

"Of course, darling."

"And Bill, will you love my firm belly, my slender legs, the taste of my love juice. . . ."

"Yes," snapped Bill. "Now will you let me get some sleep, Bruce?"

What do gays call a "quickie?"

Getting their ass in gear.

How can you tell if a woman is a bull dyke?

Find out if she rolls her own tampons.

When did the trustees of the boarding school know the entire faculty was gay?

When they couldn't separate the men from the boys.

What's a meat grinder?

A gay with a chipped tooth.

Why did the boy refuse to live with his homosexual father?

He didn't like being reared by a fag.

What's a fart?

A homosexual mating call.

What do gays call rows of urinals?

Smorgasbord.

Two lesbians were standing at the bar drinking when another girl waved from across the bar.

"Who is that chick?" one said to the other. "I'd sure like to get her spread out on my sheets."

"No you wouldn't," the other said. "She's hung like a doughnut."

What's an anal suppository?

A chastity belt for gays.

Why did they call the male hairdresser a pervert?

He went out with women.

What did the sign in the window of the gay bar read?

No chicks accepted.

How do we know there's a lot of homosexual activity in jail?

Why else would they call it "being in the can"?

The fag was hitchhiking through a small town when he was picked up by the sheriff. The lawman didn't want to lock the gay guy up, so he said, "I'm giving you two hours to blow this town."

"Fantastic!" the fag exclaimed. "Line them up and let me get started."

What's the proper way to tell a fag to have a good time on his trip?

Wish him a *buns voyage.*

What does "gay" stand for?

GOT AIDS YET?

What job do homosexuals have in the Air Force?

Tailgunners.

What do you get when you cross a homosexual with a politician?

Somebody who kisses men's hands and shakes babies.

What do you call a Jewish fairy?

A He-Blew.

Why did the gay teacher get fired?

All the reading he assigned his class was fairy tales.

What do they call gay lawyers?

Legal AIDS.

What did they call gays in Jonestown?

Kool AIDS.

Three gays were sitting in a hot tub after a torrid session of homosexual sex. Suddenly, a big wad of sperm floated to the surface of the tub.

"All right, darlings," one fag said. "Which one of you two farted?"

What do gays call hemorrhoids?

Speed bumps.

What do gays call hemorrhoids in winter?

Ski bumps.

What does A.I.D.S. stand for?

Anally Inserted Death Sentence.

How do gays spell relief?

N-O A-I-D-S.

Why do so many gay men have moustaches?

To hide the stretch marks.

A truck driver pulled over to the side of the road and picked up two homosexuals who were hitchhiking. The fags climbed into the cab, and the truck driver pulled his rig back onto the highway.

A few minutes later, the first fag said, "Excuse me, but I have to fart." He held his breath, then the truck driver heard a low "Hissssssss."

A few miles down the road, the second fag announced, "Excuse me, but I have to fart." The announcement was followed by another low "Hissssssss."

"Jesus Christ!" the truck driver exclaimed. "You fairies can't even fart like men. Listen to this." A moment later he emitted a deafening staccato machine gun burst from his ass.

"Ohhhh!" one fag exclaimed, turning to the other. "You know what we have here, Bruce? A real virgin!"

What causes homosexuality?

60% of all homosexuals are born with their sexual persuasion; 40% were sucked into it.

Chapter Seven

UTTERLY LEWD SENIOR CITIZEN JOKES

How does a man know when he's getting old?

When it takes him all night to do what he used to do all night.

Did you hear about the aging movie actress who had her face lifted so many times?

If she has it done again, she'll be a bearded lady.

The very elderly couple were listening to a religious revival on the radio. The preacher ended his stirring speech by saying, "God wants to heal you all. Just stand up, put your hand on the radio, then place the other on the part of your body that's sick."

The old woman tottered to her feet, put one hand on the radio and the other on her arthritic leg. The old man put one hand on the radio and one hand on his cock.

The old woman snapped at him, "Fred, this preacher said God would heal the sick, not raise the dead!"

How did the supermarket double its pet food sales in one week?

They instituted a senior citizen discount.

Why did the elderly woman starve to death?

She was mugged by a German shepherd on the way home from the grocery store.

What's the fanciest dish they serve in the senior citizen center?

Alpo under glass.

Why was the 18-year-old boy finally persuaded to give up his passionate affair with a ninety-year-old woman?

He was finally convinced it was merely a physical attraction.

"Don't you think I look much younger without a bra?" the decidedly aging divorcee asked her young gigilo.

"I must admit," the young hunk said, "it has drawn all the wrinkles out of your face."

An old man was talking to an old woman at the Senior Citizen Center. "You got to be careful," the geezer said. "You always get screwed when you buy a used car."

"Whoopee!" the old woman replied. "I'm going to go out and buy myself a couple."

A desperately poor, starving old woman found a few precious dollars on the street. Weak as she was, she hobbled into a supermarket to buy some food. Choosing her purchases with care, she decided to buy a dozen eggs, a loaf of day old bread, and a big bottle of ketchup she could mix with water to drink.

Clutching her food, she started home. But a half block down the street, someone bumped into her. The bag fell, the impact smashing the eggs and the ketchup. The old woman collapsed in tears.

A drunk walking down the street saw her sobbing. He stumbled over, took one look at the mess of smashed eggs and ketchup, then said, "Don't cry, lady. The way you look, that baby would have been ugly as hell anyway."

Ten-year-old Johnny and his Grandpa slept together one night so they could get up early in the morning and go fishing. In the middle of the night Grandpa shook Johnny awake and said, "Go get Grandma quick and send her in here, and you sleep in her bed."

"It's no use, Grandpa," Johnny said. "That's my dick you're squeezing!"

The old geezer walked into the health clinic and told the doctor, "You've got to do something to lower my sex drive."

The doctor took one look at the feeble man and said, "Now, now, sir. I've got the feeling your sex drive is all in your head."

"That's what I mean, sonny," the old man said. "You've got to lower it a little."

Chapter Eight

UTTERLY RAUNCHY SEX JOKES

What happened to the girl who went fishing with five guys?

She came home with a red snapper.

"Do you smoke after sex?" a man asked his gorgeous date as they took the elevator up to his apartment.

"I don't know," she replied. "I never looked down to see."

A man walked into a bar. Desperate to get laid, he picked up the only woman there, who must have weighed four hundred pounds.

They undressed and got into bed. She started writhing, then he stuck his dick in her navel and started to hump.

"Hey," she called out, "you're in the wrong hole."

"Listen, lady," he replied, "when it's this rough, any port in the storm will do."

How can women stop the population explosion?

By using their heads.

A woman turned to a man at a singles bar and asked, "Do you prefer legs with panty hose or bare legs?"

He smiled and replied, "I prefer something in between."

What's a diaphragm?"

A trampoline for sperm.

Why does a man give more expensive presents to his mistress than his wife?

When he's soft, he's hard; when he's hard, he's soft.

A midget went into a whorehouse. All of the girls looked at him and walked away. Finally, the madam made them draw lots, and one of them reluctantly walked upstairs with the little fellow.

Five minutes later a loud scream came from upstairs. The girls rushed upstairs and found the whore lying in a faint on the floor. Next to her was the naked midget, whose prick was over a foot long.

"My God," the madam stammered. "Can . . . can I touch that?"

"You can touch it," the midget said. "But for God's sake, don't suck it. I used to be six feet tall."

How did the prostitute end up in the prison hospital?

She was picked up by the fuzz.

How do they charge for designer panties?

By the pubic inch.

What's the difference between a dog and a fox?

A six pack.

A man complained to a woman at work, "I can't find a decent woman. No one I meet is fit for a pig to screw."

She looked at him icily, then replied, "If you keep talking like that, I'm sure you'll meet one who is."

A young boy walked into the bedroom while his parents were making love. He was upset, but calmed down when his father told him that Mommy and Daddy were making the baby brother he always wanted.

Two days later, however, the father came home to find his son out in the yard, crying hysterically. "What's wrong, son?" the father asked.

"You know that baby brother you and Mommy made me a couple of days ago?" the boy replied. "Well, this morning I saw the mailman eating him."

Two drunks were closing a bar one night when one said to the other, "God, I hate going home at this hour. All I want to do is sneak in and drop into bed, but my wife wakes up and nags the shit out of me for hours."

"You're doing it all wrong, trying to sneak in," the other drunk said. "I stomp in, slam the door, and scream out, 'Okay, honey, let's fuck!' My wife always pretends to be asleep."

Joe walked in the door after work and announced his arrival.

"I'm upstairs taking a douche," his wife called out.

"I told you never to talk like that," Joe said.

"What do you want," his wife replied, "good grammar or good taste?"

A man came home from a card game one night to find his mad, nagging wife in rare form. "Where have you been?" she demanded.

"It's a long story," her husband said. "But you better pack. I lost you in a card game tonight."

"How could you do such a thing?" she roared.

"It wasn't easy," the man said. "I had to fold with a royal flush."

Ten years ago, an anthropology student spent some time studying in rural regions of El Salvador. One day he was driving down the road when he saw a man on a donkey while his wife walked about ten yards behind. "Why do you do that?" he asked the man in Spanish.

"It is our age-old tradition," he was told.

Recently, the student, now a reporter, was sent back to El Salvador by his newspaper. By a strange coincidence, he found himself on the same road with the same man he'd seen ten years before. But this time the wife was walking ten yards ahead of the man on the mule.

"What happened to the custom?" he asked. "Has the tradition changed?"

"No," the man said. "Land mines."

Two guys were in the shower room of the health club. Joe noticed that Bill's cock was huge. "That's the biggest I've ever seen!" he exclaimed. "God damn, you were lucky to be born with a cock that big."

"I wasn't born this way," Bill answered. "I made it this long by rubbing it every day with butter."

Joe went home to try it. A couple of weeks later, he ran into Bill again. Bill asked, "How's it going? How much bigger is your cock?"

Joe grimaced. "I've been rubbing it every day, but it seems to be getting smaller."

"Aren't you using enough butter?"

Joe replied, "Butter's too expensive. I've been using Crisco."

"No wonder your cock's smaller," Bill said. "Crisco's shortening!"

One night a man was getting very drunk in a restaurant. He staggered back to take a piss, whipping his prick out as he went in the door. But he'd wandered into the ladies' room by mistake, surprising a woman sitting on the john.

"This is for ladies!" she shrieked. "This is for ladies!"

The drunk waved his prick at her. "So's this!" he shouted back.

A prisoner was sitting in his cell when the door clanged open and a new arrival was locked in with him.

"What are you in for?" the prisoner asked.

"Well," the guy said. "I'm not really a criminal. I just had this problem—I got a tremendous erection every time I saw a pretty girl."

"So you're in for rape?" the prisoner asked.

"No," the other con replied. "It's worse than that. My friend suggested I wear a metal jockstrap. I put one on and went to a topless night club. The shrapnel killed four dancers and a waitress."

Why is a prostitute like a chicken farmer?

Both of them earn a living raising cocks.

A man got a raise and decided to buy a scope for his hunting rifle. He went to a gun shop outside of town, and the clerk fitted a scope to his weapon. "This scope is so good you can read the name on the mailbox of my house way up on that hill," the clerk said.

The man looked through the scope and a big grin spread over his face.

"What's so funny?" the clerk asked.

"I see a naked woman and a naked man through the window."

"That can't be!" the clerk exclaimed. "My wife's at work."

He grabbed the scope, took a look for himself, and to his chagrin, he found the hunter was right.

Furious, he gave the rifle back to the hunter and said, "The scope is yours for nothing if you take these two bullets. Shoot my wife in the head, then shoot off that guy's dick."

The hunter, looking through the scope, said, "I think I can do that in one shot."

The 16-year-old girl came home one day and told her mother she was pregnant.

"That's terrible!" the mother exclaimed.

"And it's all your fault," the girl said angrily.

"Why is it my fault?" the startled mother asked. "I told you about the birds and the bees."

"But you never taught me how to give a decent blow job."

Why is sex like the game of bridge?

You either need a good partner or a good hand.

A traveling salesman picked up a woman in a small town bar and took her for a ride in the country. When they got passionate, he discovered he didn't have a rubber, so he wrapped his silk tie around his dick.

Years later, he found himself in that same town again. He saw a young boy who looked a lot like him. "Well, you're a handsome fellow," the salesman said.

"Mommy says I had to be," the boy said. "I was strained through a silk tie."

"Daddy must be going to buy a real small car," the boy said to his mother one day.

"How do you know that, dear?" the mother asked.

"Well, I was looking in his coat pocket and I found these tiny inner tubes."

What's the definition of frustration?

When your date puts her bra on backwards, and it fits.

Bill went over to his fiancée's apartment and told her he had to break off the engagement to marry somebody else.

His fiancée immediately broke out in tears. When her sobbing subsided, she demanded to know, "Can this woman cook like I can?"

"No," Bill said.

"Can she buy you wonderful, expensive presents like I can?"

"No."

"Well, then, is it sex?"

"No," Bill said, "nobody makes love as well as you."

"Then what can this woman do?"

Bill replied sadly, "Sue me for child support."

Why don't bankers suffer from premature ejaculation?

Because they know there's a penalty for early withdrawal.

Shortly after dinner one Sunday, the couple got into an argument. The wife complained to her husband that he wasn't virile enough—her friend's husband satisfied her five times nightly. Stung, the husband said he'd do the same thing for her.

He managed twice in a row before taking a nap. He took another nap after the third time, barely made it through the fourth, napped again before the fifth, then finally fell asleep.

When he woke up, the clock read 9:15. He didn't get into the office until 10:00 a.m. Immediately, he went into the boss to apologize.

"It's not your being late this morning," the boss groused. "I just want to know where you were Monday, Tuesday, and Wednesday."

A guy had a few too many at the bar, and ended up picking up a woman. By the time they got up in the room, he'd sobered up enough to discover she was the ugliest woman he'd ever seen in his life. Unfortunately, he was so horny he thought he'd die if he didn't get laid.

He sat thinking for a moment, then picked up the phone.

"What are you doing?" the woman asked.

"I'm calling room service for a bottle of booze and a paper bag."

"You mean a bottle of booze in a paper bag," she said.

"No," he said. "The bag is for your head."

How can you tell kids learn about sex early in Hollywood?

It's the only place where kids have skateboards with built-in mattresses.

The bride had been a virgin until her wedding night. The next morning, her husband woke up to find her crying.

"What's wrong, dear?" he asked. "Did I hurt you last night?"

She shook her head, still sobbing. "No," she said. Then, pointing to his dick, she added, "But look at your thing. One night, and we used it all up."

A motorist looked to his left and saw a motorcycle patrolman motioning him to pull over. When he pulled the car to a stop, the cop came up to him and said, "Hey, Mac. Your wife fell out of the car a couple of miles back."

"Thank God!" the man cried. "I thought I'd gone deaf."

"How's your new bride?" a man asked a friend whom he hadn't seen in a while.

The man grimaced. "I'm afraid I married a nymphomaniac. A couple of weeks ago I took her to a club with a three man combo, and the next night I caught her in bed with the three musicians. Last week, I took her to a basketball game, and the next night I caught her in bed with all five guys on the starting team."

"That's awful," the friend said.

"That isn't the worst. Tomorrow we're going to see the Saint Patrick's Day parade."

A man walked into an appliance store and asked the price of a 25″ remote controlled color television set.

"One dollar," the clerk replied.

"You've got to be kidding."

"Look, Mac," the clerk said, "do you want it or not?"

Of course, the customer gave him a dollar. On the way out with his incredible bargain, the customer saw a big frost-free refrigerator with automatic ice maker. "How much for that?" he asked the clerk.

"Fifty cents," came the reply.

The customer forked over the half dollar, saying, "What the hell is going on here?"

"Nothing is going on here," the clerk snapped. "But my boss is at my house with my wife. And what he's doing to her, I'm doing to his business."

Why wouldn't the hooker screw any sailors?

The doctor put her on a salt-free diet.

A guy picked up a girl in a singles bar, took her home, hopped into bed, and said, "Baby, you're in for a treat. I'm going to fuck your brains out."

A half hour later the girl pulled a feather out of the pillow and began tapping him on the head.

"What are you doing?" he asked.

"Well, lover boy," yawned the girl, "in your terms, I'm beating your brains out."

The man was impatient to get on with lovemaking, but the woman kept slowing him down. "Patience, darling," she said. "Foreplay is an art."

"Well," the guy grunted, "if you don't get your canvas arranged soon, I'm going to spill my paint."

Two actresses were talking while waiting to audition. One bragged to the other, "I insured my tits with Lloyds of London for $1,000,000."

"Congratulations!" said the other. "What did you buy with the money you collected?"

A self-proclaimed smoothie went over to the gorgeous-looking girl sitting at the bar and said, "Hey, baby. I'd sure like to get into those pants of yours."

"No chance," the woman snapped. "One asshole in there is enough."

A little boy was taking a bath with his sister for the first time. She noticed his penis and said, "What's that? Can I touch it?"

"Don't you dare!" the boy cried angrily.

"Why not?"

"I'm not crazy," the boy said. "You must have touched yours and look what happened. The whole thing fell off."

Why did the very curvacious young WAVE decide to re-enlist in the Navy?

Her re-enlistment gift was a 13″ Admiral.

"I haven't found a guy with the right size cock," a woman confided to her friend.

"What's the problem?" the friend asked.

"Either the guy is so small I want to scream, or too large so that I have to."

A guy away at a convention spent a few too many hours at the hotel bar. Finally, he stumbled over to a woman and grabbed her hard between the legs. She turned and slapped him.

"Sorry," the drunk said, sobering slightly. "For a minute, I thought you were my wife."

"You're nothing but a stupid, goddamn sot!" the woman said angrily.

"Jesus," the drunk said, "you sound exactly like my wife, too."

A businessman spent half an hour in a bar bragging to a hooker about how long his cock was. Finally, they struck a financial deal and retired to a hotel room.

When he had his clothes off, the businessman jumped on the hooker, inserted his penis, and cried, "There, it's in. Open your mouth so I can see it."

"Open my mouth," the hooker scoffed. "Why don't you try wiggling your ass so I can feel it."

Why are women like screen doors?

Once they get banged a few times, they tend to loosen up.

Two men in their mid-thirties were sitting in a bar relating their most embarrassing moments. One confided to the other that he'd been caught hiding in the closet watching his parents screw.

"That's not so bad," the other said. "A lot of kids do that."

"Yeah," the first man replied, "but I got caught last night."

One starlet arrived at a friend's house, saying, "Sorry I'm so late. I had a rare in-depth audition this afternoon."

"What's an in-depth audition?"

"A producer with nine inches."

Why is it safer to suck on a Florida orange than a California orange?

Because a lot of California oranges suck back.

The new husband and bride were in bed, when the man said, "Honey, anytime you wake up and want sex, you don't have to say a word. Just reach over and pull on my penis a couple of times."

"And if I don't want sex?"

"Pull on it forty or fifty times," the man said.

What's a meat locker?

A male chastity belt.

What do they call the new sex club in New York City that attracts women who are real dogs?

Pluto's Retreat.

A woman began bringing in extra income, but she refused to tell her husband where her part time job was. While she was away one Saturday morning, her husband took their young daughter to the market. When they got to the cereal section, he asked her what kind she liked.

"I still like Cheerios," the young girl replied. "But I heard Mommy say on the phone that now she's eating something called Trix."

"Where did I come from, Mommy?" the little girl asked.

"Why, dear," the mother replied, "you came in a bucket."

The little girl toddled into the living room and asked her father, "Daddy, Mommy said I came from a bucket. Is that really true?"

The father grimaced, musing on his wife's anatomy. "Yes, dear," he said, "that's really about the size of it."

"I used to have a bad case of penis envy," the young secretary confided to a friend.

"How did you get over it?"

The pretty young thing replied, "I started work, and so many of the men in the office were willing to share theirs."

The Southern hillbilly stationed overseas in the Army was delighted to hear that his wife was pregnant.

"But you've been in Germany alone for nearly two years!" a friend exclaimed.

"So?" the hillbilly said. "There's two years 'tween my brother and me."

Why do prostitutes seldom vote in elections?

They don't care who gets in.

A pretty young secretary was telling her girlfriend that she spent the night with a much older executive from the company.

"That's terrible," her friend said. "How could you sleep with him?"

"I had to," the secretary said. "He told the desk clerk I was his wife."

Two drunks were stumbling along the street after closing hours, both of them having struck out in their attempt to pick up a woman.

They careened around a corner and noticed a mailbox sitting beside a fire alarm mounted on a telephone pole.

"Wow!" one exclaimed. "Look at those two babes!"

"Forget it," the other said. "The fat one in blue doesn't say a word, and if you touch the one in the red coat, she screams her head off."

What's the definition of an idiot?

A guy who rips a girl's bra off and starts biting her ear.

A hooker was driving along in the country on her way to an expensive resort when her car broke down. She walked to a farmhouse. The owner said she could stay the night if she helped with the evening chores.

The hooker agreed, and went out to the barn with the farmer's daughter. The young girl showed the whore the cow's udder and asked if she could milk. "You kidding?" the hooker said. "That's my profession."

A few minutes later, the farmer's daughter asked the hooker how she was doing.

"I can't figure it out," the hooker said. "How long do you have to pull these things before they get hard?"

Why do newborn babies cry when they're slapped?

Because they're too little to swear.

Did you hear about the new TV show that features army doctors trying to treat King Kong?

It's called M*A*S*H*E*D.

How do you protect yourself from fallout?

Put it back in and take shorter strokes.

The recently married couple split up shortly after the ceremony. The trouble started when the husband arrived home from work and found his lovely young wife lying on the couch, naked, with her legs spread wide open.

"What's for dinner?" the husband asked.

"Pussy," she replied.

"Shit," the husband spat. "I had that for lunch."

A smooth operator walked into a crowded singles bar. He ordered a drink, surveyed the scene, then spotted a beautiful stranger at the far corner of the bar. He casually and confidently strode over, slid onto the stool next to her, then said, "Hi. I'll bet we're here for the same reason."

"Oh, great," the girl exclaimed. "Let's pick up some of these cunts and take them home."

Why is being in the Army like a blowjob?

The closer you get to discharge, the better you feel.

What's the definition of premature ejaculation?

A spoil-spurt.

Two guys were having lunch, when one boasted to the other, "Last night I got the greatest blowjob in the history of the world. No other girl could suck cock like that."

"Come on," his friend said sarcastically, "you're always saying that."

"It was different this time," the first man said. "That girl sucked so hard that when I woke up this morning, I had to use two hands to pull the sheets out of my asshole."

A traveling salesman couldn't believe his luck as the farmer's wife wriggled out of her pants.

"I'll be damned!" the man exclaimed as her bush came into view. Her brown pubic hair was neatly trimmed in a beaver tail, with a neat row of gray fur stretching down the middle.

"Eat me, baby. Eat my beaver," the woman whispered hungrily as she lay back on the bed. The salesman ripped off his clothes and buried his nose between her vaginal lips. Then, a few seconds later, he jumped up and began to put his clothes back on.

"What's the matter?" the woman asked.

"Lady," the salesman said, "I may be from the city, but I know the difference between beaver and skunk!"

A man went into a drugstore and asked the pharmacist if they had any black rubbers.

"I'm afraid we don't," the man said. "But we have the normal ones. They'll do the same job."

"No, they won't," the customer said. "You see, a friend of mine died recently. I want to dress right when I mourn with his widow."

Coming home early from work one afternoon, a man found his wife naked in bed, breathing heavily and visibly distressed.

"Linda, what's the matter?" he asked.

"I . . . I don't know," she stammered. "Maybe I'm having a heart attack."

The man rushed downstairs to call a doctor. He was dialing when his daughter hurried in, shouting, "Daddy! Daddy! There's a naked man in the closet."

The husband rushed upstairs, opened the closet door, and found his best friend inside. "For God's sake, Ed," the man said. "My wife's in the bedroom having a heart attack, and you've got to sneak around scaring the kids."

A prostitute propositioned a hillbilly on his first visit to the big city. She offered to screw him for $25. "I'm sorry," he said. "All I've got is five dollars."

After a bit of negotiation, the hooker took him into a dark alley and allowed him to get a look at her pussy. He lit some matches, then exclaimed, "God damn, that looks good. But ma'am, can I ask you a question?"

"Okay," the whore replied.

"Can you really piss through all that hair?"

"Sure."

"Then you better start," the hillbilly said, "'cause you're on fire."

Chapter Nine

UTTERLY DISGUSTING

Why does Ronald Reagan eat jelly beans?

So he can come in ten delicious colors.

What's the definition of perpetual motion?

Helen Keller looking up a number in the phone book.

How did Helen Keller's parents punish her?

They put a toilet seat on the stove.

Where did Helen Keller vacation?

Blind man's bluff.

What's a Helen Keller doll?

You wind it up and it walks into walls.

Why did Helen Keller's dog walk in front of a car?

You would too, if your name was "Urrggggh."

How did Helen Keller go crazy?

Trying to read a stucco wall.

What's a sadist?

A person who's kind to a masochist.

A man went to an air-conditioned dinner theater and devoured a huge meal before the show. By the middle of the first act, he had to take a dump. He got up in the darkness, found a stairway, and went up the next flight.

The second floor was filled with stored equipment. But the man had to go so bad he couldn't wait. He spotted a hole in the floor and he couldn't resist. He went over, squatted, and relieved himself.

When he went downstairs, however, he saw people pouring out of the theater, many of them smelling horribly. "Is the play over?" he asked a man.

"Yeah," the man said, "a few minutes ago the shit really hit the fan."

A butcher had a daughter whom he couldn't marry off. The girl just wasn't interested in any of her suitors, and the butcher stayed up sleepless many nights wondering what he could do.

One night, the butcher heard noises down in his shop. He got out of bed and tiptoed down the stairs to see his daughter masturbating furiously with liverwurst. The butcher turned and went back up to bed.

The next day the butcher was working in the shop with his daughter when a customer pointed to the display case and said, "I'd like to buy that liverwurst."

"I'm afraid that's not for sale," the butcher said. "That's my son-in-law."

A man died from dysentery. When the undertaker got the corpse, his ass was still oozing, so he put a cork in it and set about his work.

The wake was scheduled for 10:00 a.m. the next morning. The four pallbearers arrived to carry the open casket down to the viewing room. His best friend Murphy was weeping as he picked up the remains of his buddy.

But when the casket was moved, the cork slipped out and shit came raining down on Murphy's head.

"What the hell did you do?" the undertaker asked as he came running up.

"I don't know," Murphy said as he dropped the casket. "But if that bastard can shit, he can walk."

A traveling salesman was forced to seek shelter at a remote farmhouse during a raging blizzard. The farmer said he had relatives visiting, and there was no empty bed. The salesman offered him $10, and the farmer reluctantly agreed he could climb in bed with his daughter.

The salesman went up to bed with a huge grin on his face, but he came down the next morning frowning. "Boy, your daughter's cold," he said to the farmer.

"I know," the farmer said. "We have to wait until it stops snowing to bury her."

A very proper young lady was out riding on a moonlit night, escorted by a stable boy who was assigned to see to her safety. After an hour's jaunt, they got off their mounts for a rest. Immediately, one of the horses dropped its penis and began pissing.

Embarrassed, the young lady pointed to the sky and asked, "Where is the Big Dipper?"

"Miss," the stable lad said, "you don't want no dipper. That horse piss ain't fit to drink."

"Boy, my wife's impossible to deal with when she's got her period," a man complained to a friend.

"Really?"

"I'll tell you how bad it is," the man said. "Last night I arrived home from work exhausted. All I asked her to do was make me a drink. But she got so teed off that she handed me a Bloody Mary with a string in it."

What's the difference in the way men and women piss?

A man holds his equipment when he wants to piss, and a woman holds her equipment when she doesn't.

Two women were sitting in the waiting room of an abortion clinic. One saw that the other was knitting what looked like a baby bonnet. It bothered her so much that she turned and scolded, "How could you knit a bonnet when you're about to have an abortion?"

"Oh," the knitter said, "it's not a bonnet. It's a body bag."

A grandmother visited her slovenly daughter-in-law. She was appalled to see how fat her little grandson had become.

"Really, Agnes," she said to the daughter-in-law, "you've got to stop feeding Billy all that junk food."

"He doesn't eat junk food," the mother said. "He's that fat because he won't stop picking his nose and eating it."

What's pile carpeting?

Hair on hemorrhoids.

Little Billy's enlightened mother thought he was old enough to learn some of the facts of life. One day she took off her clothes, pointed to her cunt, and said, "Billy, that's where you came from."

"Wow!" Billy exclaimed. He ran out on the street, a huge grin on his face. One of his friends saw him, and asked why he was so happy.

Billy measured out an inch or so between his thumb and forefinger. "I came that close to being born a turd."

The Polish guy opened a diner, but he wasn't doing any business until he advertised a special pizza for $10. One family in the neighborhood tried it, then spread the word fast.

By the end of the week, families were lined up to get pizzas. "I don't understand it," one guy said to the Polack as he waited. "You're not even Italian. How do you make such good pizza?"

"Easy," the Polack said. "I buy the dough ready made. Then I go to Little Italy and get a few Italians to throw up on it."

A man went into his neighborhood deli to get a few groceries. He asked the owner, "Where's that nice kid you had working for you?"

The owner grimaced. "I had to fire him. I caught him jerking off in the back room."

"Isn't that harsh?" the man asked. "All boys jerk off."

"Yeah," the owner said. "But not all of them do it in my cole slaw."

A drunk flopped down on the bar stool so hard that the cushion let out a huge explosion. Startled, he yelled at the bartender, "Hey buddy, this stool just farted."

"No, it didn't," the bartender replied. "That's just air being forced out of the cushion."

"Yeah, sure," the drunk groused. The bartender saw him grimace so hard his face turned bright red. Then the drunk leaped off the stool and started out of the bar.

Suspicious, the bartender leaned over to see a large pile of shit on the cushion.

"Hey," he yelled at the man. "Why did you do that?"

"I wasn't going to let it shit on me first," the departing drunk hollered back.

What's marijuana?

Grass that can mow down a gardener.

What has President Reagan done for the country?

About what panty hose did for fingerfucking.

"How did your son like boy scout camp?" a man asked a friend.

The friend beamed, "He was named camper of the month."

"For winning the most merit badges?" the man asked.

"He's much more clever than that," the friend bragged. "He designed an artificial vagina out of his camping gear."

What's the definition of chutzpah?

A guy who can't get a date showing up at an orgy with an artificial vagina.

The morning after his birthday party, a man woke up not only to find he had an awful hangover, but his wife wasn't speaking to him. It was hours before he could ask, "Why are you so mad at me?"

"You made a total fool of yourself," she snapped. "You were so drunk that when I brought out the cake, you pulled down your pants and tried to blow out the candles with a fart."

"My God!" the embarrassed man exclaimed.

"That isn't the worst," his wife said. "When you tried, you shit on the cake instead."

A woman was eating with her new boyfriend at an expensive restaurant when she inadvertently let out a huge fart. Embarrassed, she turned to the waiter and said, "Please stop that immediately."

"Of course, madame," the very professional waiter said, "which way was it headed?"

Did you hear about the woman crawling through the desert with a douche bag?

She was moaning, "Vinegar and water. Give me vinegar and water."

Who was Tinker Bell's abortionist?

Captain Hook.

"Tell me, darling," an executive said to his devoted mistress, "what would you do if you found yourself pregnant and abandoned?"

"Oh, that would be awful," the young thing exclaimed. "I think I'd kill myself."

"Good girl," the executive said.

Why is a woman's pussy like a warm toilet seat?

They're both nice, but you always wonder who was there before you.

A woman went to the doctor for an exam. When she disrobed, the doctor was astounded to see that she had one perfectly normal tit, and one tit that was so stretched out it touched the floor.

"What happened?" the doctor said.

"My husband likes to suck on that tit."

"So?"

The woman replied, "We have bunk beds."

A young girl went to a doctor and complained that people kept telling her that her pussy stank. She said that couldn't be true, because when she bent over, she couldn't smell a thing.

The doctor conducted a complete examination. When he was through, he said, "I'm afraid you need an operation."

"On my pussy?" the girl asked.

"No," the doctor said. "On your nose."

Why are women amazing?

They give milk without eating hay, they bleed without getting cut, and they bury bones without digging holes.

What's the definition of bar stool?

What Davy Crockett stepped in when he went hunting.

A woman was visiting her friend when she noticed papers on the floor in the kitchen. She assumed her friend hadn't had time to clean up until the friend's three-year-old son walked over and shit on the papers.

"Did you see that?" the woman asked, shocked.

"Isn't he good?" the friend exclaimed. "He had such a bad reaction to toilet training we thought this was a wonderful first step."

A man went to a brothel very late one night, and he had to settle for the oldest, ugliest whore in the place. He was so disgusted all he could do was shit in her face. To his surprise, he really enjoyed it. The next few nights, he came back, deliberately asked for the old whore, and shit in her face again.

After a couple of weeks, however, the thrill wore off. One night he came in, asked for a young girl, and fucked her. On the way out, the old whore came up to him, crying her eyes out. "What's the matter?" she wailed. "Don't you love me anymore?"

Did you hear about the sperm bank that came up with a new freezing method?

Now their product tastes like fresh squeezed.

The foreman at the dairy was livid when he found the new milkman beating off into a milk bottle.

"What in the hell do you think you're doing?" the foreman demanded.

"Providing customer service, just as we were trained," the man replied. "One of my customers asked for extra cream."

A man complained to his friend, "I think that girl I picked up in the bar was way under age."

"Why?" the friend asked. "Was she inexperienced?"

"God, no. She gave me a fantastic blow job. The trouble was, I woke up this morning with bubble gum all over my cock."

An eight-year-old boy was walking home with a girl in his class when he said, "Jenny, you're the first girl I ever loved."

"Shit," she replied. "If there's anything I don't need, it's another beginner."

To save money, the Army commissioned an efficiency expert to find a way to cut down on the cost of toilet paper. He studied the problem for a month, then came up with the solution that would save $10 million. He produced a toilet paper dispenser that would only issue one piece at a time. Each tissue had a one inch hole in the middle.

The instructions read: "For use, pull off tissue and remove the perforated center. Insert finger through the resulting hole and wipe the soiled area. Grasp the underside of the tissue and use to clean the finger. If necessary, use the remaining tissue to clean underneath the nail."

A man went to a medium and asked if there were any golf courses in heaven. The medium unveiled a crystal ball, put her hands on it, and meditated for a few minutes.

"Well?" the impatient man finally asked.

"I'm getting a strong message," the medium said. "I've got some good news and some bad news."

"What's the good news?"

"There's a championship quality course in heaven, more challenging than any course in this world."

"Great!" the golfer said. "What could possibly be the bad news?"

"You tee off on that course tomorrow at 8:00 a.m."

Fred's wife used some gasoline to clean up some grease she'd spilled on the kitchen floor, then she dumped the rest in the toilet.

A little while later, Fred came home, went into the john, lit a cigarette, then dropped the burning match. An instant later came a loud explosion.

His wife ran into the room, screaming hysterically, "Oh Fred, I'm sorry. I put gasoline in the bowl and forgot to flush."

Fred was crawling around on his hands and knees. "To hell with apologizing," he shouted. "And help me find the thing I was peeing with."

The race car driver picked up a girl after the race, went home with her, and took her to bed. He fell asleep, only to wake up suddenly when she smacked him in the face.

"What's the matter?" the driver said. "Wasn't I okay when we screwed?"

"It was after you fell asleep that you got in trouble," the angry woman said. "In your sleep, you felt my tits and mumbled, 'What perfect headlights.' Then you felt my thighs and murmured, 'What a smooth finish.'"

"What's wrong with that?" the driver asked.

"Nothing. But then you felt my pussy and yelled, 'Who the hell left the garage door open?'"

A man walked into a bar, desperate to get laid. The only woman in the bar was decidedly over the hill. But after a couple of stiff drinks, the man couldn't resist putting the move on her.

The woman readily agreed. They left the bar and checked into a local motel. The man grimaced when he took off her bra and saw how saggy her tits were, but he persevered. He took off her skirt, then said, "Hey, babe. There's lint all over your panties."

"That ain't lint," the woman said. "Those are maggots."

In rural parts of Tennessee, if you get a girl pregnant, you have to marry her. With this in mind, the parents of a young girl timed their daughter's monthly cycle, then found an eligible young man, invited him over, and conveniently left the house.

Sure enough, the couple were in the sack in no time. The parents came back in the house and sat in the living room discussing what to name the baby. "Maybe Lana Lou if it's a girl," the mother said. "Or Billy Bob if it's a boy?"

"Or Houdini," the boy said as he came out of the bedroom swinging a used rubber. "He'd have to be Houdini if he figures a way to get out of here."

An Indian chief walked into the drugstore complaining, "Rubbers you sell me no good. Chief go 'Ugh,' squaw go 'Ugh,' rubbers go 'BOOM.'"

The druggist answered, "Here's the strongest rubber made."

The chief agreed to use it. But he came back to say, "Rubber no good. Chief go 'Ugh,' squaw go 'Ugh,' rubber go 'BOOM.'"

The frustrated druggist went into the back room, welded shut one end of an iron pipe, stretched a balloon over it, and went back out to give it to the chief.

The following day the squaw showed up. "Rubber you sell chief too good. Chief go 'Ugh,' squaw go 'Ugh,' chief's balls go 'BOOM.'"

Why did the antique dealer make love to the menstruating woman?

Because he loved period pieces.

Is Nancy Reagan frigid?

It's hard to tell for sure, but on a hot day in Washington, they cool the White House by putting her in the window and letting the breeze flow between her legs.

A guest in a small town hotel had to go to the bathroom in the middle of the night. He wandered down the dark hall, but took a wrong turn. Instead of the bathroom, he stopped outside of the bridal suite, where a couple were going at it.

The guest turned the doorknob a couple of times, but found it locked. He began to rattle it harder when the exasperated groom called out, "What do you want?"

"You should know," the guest replied. "If you're not using both holes in there, I want to use the other one."

What did Little Red Riding Hood say when she walked into her grandmother's house and lifted the sheet?

"My, Grandmother, what a big clitoris you have!"

Some guys were sitting around at the Ku Klux Klan meeting talking about their Army experiences. One guy complained that he'd been stationed in a remote part of Alaska for over a year.

"Were there any females around?" he was asked.

"Only polar bears. Thank God they were white."

"Just how do you plan to use this artificial vagina?" asked the sex shop proprietor.

"That's none of your business!" the angry customer retorted.

"Sorry, sir," the proprietor said. "I'm just trying to help you out. I don't have to charge you sales tax if it's a food item."

What's a vibrator?

A toy for twats.

The owners of two general stores ran into each other at a tavern. They started talking business. One asked the other, "How do you manage to sell so many lawnmowers?"

"Clever salesmanship," the other replied. "When someone comes in to buy a bag of grass seed, I point out that when the grass grows, they'll need a lawnmower. That kind of selling works with any product."

The first owner vowed to try it. When he opened his store the next day, the first customer was a woman who asked for a box of tampons. He gave her the box, and then asked if she needed a lawnmower.

"Why would I need a lawnmower?" the woman asked.

"Well," replied the store owner, "if you can't fuck, you might as well cut the grass."

An old lady tottered into the main branch of Chase Manhattan Bank every single Friday afternoon just before 3 and handed the teller $100,000 in cash. That was so remarkable that word filtered all the way up to David Rockefeller, chairman of the board of the bank. One Friday Rockefeller came down to the main floor to talk to the old woman.

"Where do you get your money?" Rockefeller asked the spry senior citizen after she made her customary deposit.

"I gamble," the woman said.

"I don't believe it," Rockefeller said. "I consider myself a gambler, like every big businessman, but sometimes even I lose. How do you win $100,000 every week?"

"I make the right bets," the old woman said. Then she asked, "Would you be interested in a wager?"

"It depends," Rockefeller said.

"Well, I'll bet you $100,000 that next Friday at exactly 3 p.m., your balls are square."

Rockefeller immediately took the bet. But the amount was so big that all week long he consistently reached into his pants to check his balls. By the time he felt them at 2:55 Friday, he was sure he won.

A minute later, the old lady walked into his office, followed by a wealthy looking old gentleman.

"Well," Rockefeller said, "I guess I won."

"Considering the amount involved," the old woman said, "do you mind if I check?"

Rockefeller reluctantly consented and dropped his pants as the old woman fondled him.

"Well," he said. "You finally lost $100,000."

"Yes," the old woman said. "But I have a deposit of $100,000 to make." Pointing to the other man, she explained, "I bet him $200,000 that at 3 on Friday, I'd be feeling Rockefeller's balls."

An Italian girl saw a girlfriend in a store buying a false beard. "What are you doing with that?" she asked as her friend tried the beard on.

"Can't you tell?" the girl asked. "I've been invited to a costume party, and I'm going as my armpit."

What's the definition of a crying shame?

A Puerto Rican school bus going over a cliff with four empty seats.

What's green and sits on the toilet?

A girl scout doing her duty.

A guy walked into a bar one night shaking his head.
"What's the matter?" a friend asked. "Didn't you have a good time with that broad you took home?"
"Naw," the guy said. "She had the biggest cunt you ever saw."
"What did you do?"
"What could I do?" the guy asked. "I threw in a penny, made a wish, and sent her home."

How did Captain Hook die?

He wiped with the wrong hand.

What do you get when you mix Kodak film with Preparation H?

A cure for Polaroids.

What's worse than having your doctor tell you you have VD?

Having your dentist tell you.

What's the best way to get rid of crabs?

Find a cocksucker with a craving for seafood.

One of the networks was looking for an emcee to host a new game show called GROSS OUT. After interviewing dozens of identical jokers, a new guy was ushered in.

"What can you do?" the producer demanded.

The guy took his hat off and vomited in it.

"So?" the producer said. "What's so special about that?"

The guy laughed. "Got a straw?"

What do tampons and eye drops have in common?

They both get the red out.

A ragged, bearded castaway, alone for years on a desert island, suddenly began shouting, "A ship! A ship! It's heading this way! And I bet," he went on talking to himself, "there's a gorgeous blonde onboard. With big, bouncing boobs. And shapely hips. Not to mention a round, smooth ass. I can just taste her hot lips as our naked bodies come together. I can . . ."

By then the fellow had a throbbing hard on. He grabbed himself and began masturbating furiously. "I gotcha now, you bastard!" he exclaimed. "There ain't no fucking ship!"

What's a wife?

An attachment you screw on the bed to get the housework done.

Little Red Riding Hood was walking through the woods one day with her basket of goodies when all of a sudden a big bad wolf jumped out from behind a tree. The wolf said, "Little Red Riding Hood, drop those scarlet britches—I'm going to fuck you."

Little Red Riding Hood reached into her basket, pulled out a pistol, and said, "Oh, no, you're not, asshole. You're gonna eat me just like the story says."

A not-too-bright young lady went into an employment agency looking for work. She sat down with a counselor and he began filling out the necessary forms.

"What's your name?" he asked.

"Maggie Brown," she answered. "M-A-G-G-I-E B-R-O-W-N."

"No," he said, "I need your whole name."

"Oh," she replied. "Vagina. V-A-G-I-N-A."

What's feminine deodorant spray?

Around-the-cock protection.

What's better than a "10"?

A "7" that swallows.

Two country girls were walking down the lane. One girl asked the other, "How old are you?"

"I don't know," the girl replied. "My mother lost my birth certificate. She thinks I'm either 11 or 14."

The other girl thought a moment, then asked, "What's the best thing you ever had in your mouth?"

"Mmmmm. I guess that would be a big slice of apple pie with vanilla ice cream."

"Then you're 11," the other girl said.

Three coeds were talking about a guy each had dated in the recent past.

The first said, "He thinks he's pretty cool, so I decided to teach him a lesson. When I went to his room, I found his condoms lying on the table. I stuffed them into a sock so he couldn't find them. Boy, that really cramped his style."

The second girl said, "I thought that a sock was a really weird place to keep rubbers. Since it was my period, I didn't worry about getting laid, but I wanted to play a joke on him. I took the rubbers, punctured each one, then put them back in the drawer where he could find them."

The third coed fainted.

Two buddies at the bar were comparing the sexual behavior of their spouses.

"Hey," one said, "does your wife close her eyes when you're pumping away at her?"

"She sure does," the other replied. "She just can't stand to watch me having a good time."

What did the elephant say when he saw the naked man lying on the ground?

"How can you eat with that thing?"

Two men were brought into court for fighting. One fellow said, "Your Honor, I had to hit that guy. He said my wife was the ugliest, dirtiest, smelliest, hairiest old whore in town."

The judge replied, "Well, that's terrible. Why don't you bring your wife here to testify against him, too?"

The man looked suddenly uncomfortable. "Uh . . . well . . . Your Honor, before I do, I'd like to know one thing. Will it hurt my case if he's telling the truth?"

A drunk wandered down the street looking for a whorehouse. But he stumbled into a podiatrist's office by mistake.

When he walked in, the nurse told him to go behind a curtain and put it through the hole. He did as he was told. The nurse screamed, "That's not a foot!"

Frank yelled back, "I didn't know there was a minimum!"

What's artificial insemination?

A technical knock-up

What do you call a virgin on a waterbed?

A cherry float.

What's a lap dog?

An ugly woman who gives head.

What did the nymphomaniac like best about joining the nudist colony?

The contact with new members.

A couple of squirrels were going through the park looking for a convenient tree where they could have dinner and spend the night. Inadvertently, however, one ran up the skirt of a girl who was wearing no panties. A moment later, he came back down, a look of disgust on his face.

"That tree's no good?" his friend asked.

"The worst. Bare limbs, no nuts, and the nest is all wet and sticky!"

When does the Jolly Green Giant go "Ho, ho, ho!"?

When someone in the valley starts playing with his little green sprout.

Where did inflation begin?

In the Garden of Eden. Inflation started with Adam and ended up in Eve.

What happened to the man who deflowered the virgin?

He got arrested for breaking and entering.

What's the definition of an orgasm?

A gland finale.

A woman hailed a cab late one night. When the taxi pulled up in front of her apartment building, however, she discovered she'd forgotten her purse. "Hey," she said to the cabbie, "I don't have any money. Will you settle for taking the fare out in trade?"

As she spoke, she lifted up her skirt, pulled down her panties, and spread her legs wide to display her cunt.

The cabbie put the taxi in park, turned around to look, then grimaced. "Lady," he said, "haven't you got anything smaller?"

Why don't Polacks eat M & M's?

Because they're too hard to peel.

Why can't you give a Puerto Rican a blow job?

Because you can't give a Puerto Rican any kind of job.

What's the difference between a Polish girl and a bowling ball?

You can only fit three fingers in a bowling ball.

A Polack bought a farm outside a small Alabama community. On Saturday, he went into town and asked some of the locals hanging out on Main Street what they did for fun.

"Why, we go over to the bowling alley and beat up Niggers," came the reply.

That night, the Polack came into the bowling alley just as a group of blacks came in. Sure enough, the whites began attacking them. The Polack picked up a baseball bat, and started smashing bowling balls.

"What are you doing?" a redneck yelled.

"You get the Niggers," the Polack said. "I'll get rid of these eggs."

A Jewish salesman on his lunch hour walked into a garment district whorehouse. Too cheap to buy a rubber, he took a label from one of his samples and wrapped it around the end of his dick. He got so excited, however, the label fell off while he was pumping away.

The whore's next customer was a Polack. He climbs on and reaches climax. But when he pulls his dick out, he notices something stuck to it. He grabs it and reads, "Roth and Stein, Fine Men's Wear."

"God damn!" he swears. "Those Jews advertise everywhere."

What do you do with a dead Texan who's too big for his coffin?

Give him an enema and put him in a shoebox.

Why don't Arabs get hemorrhoids?

Because they're such perfect assholes.

What's the newest Vietnamese cookbook?

101 Ways to Wok Your Dog.

What's the difference between Polish pussy and a bowling ball?

If you try hard enough, you could probably eat a bowling ball.

A Polack was suffering from hemorrhoids, so the doctor prescribed suppositories.

A week later, the Pole complained to his doctor that they didn't help at all.

"Have you been taking them every day?" the doctor asked.

"What do you think I've been doing?" the Polack retorted indignantly. "Shoving them up my ass?"

An Italian, a Jew and a Polack were talking in a bar when the question came up, "Why is there a head on a man's penis?"

The Italian said, "To give a man more pleasure."

The Jew said, "You're wrong. The head gives the woman more pleasure."

"No, no, you're both wrong," the Polack said. "A penis has a head to keep your hand from slipping off."

Two Polacks were out hunting rabbits one day when one turned to the other and said, "I've got to take a shit."

"Just go behind the tree over there," his friend said.

"But I don't have any toilet paper," the first Polack said.

"Listen," his friend said. "Use a dollar."

The first Polack ran off toward the bushes. A few minutes later he came back with shit all over his hand and arm.

"Hey," his friend said, "I thought I told you to use a dollar."

"I did," the Polack replied. "Three quarters, two dimes, and a nickel."

An American businessman spent a lot of time in Rome. A devout Catholic, he tried for years to get a private audience with the Pope. When his request was finally granted, he reverently approached his Holiness and kissed his ring. After the Pope had blessed him, the businessman said, "Your Holiness, I want you to know this has been the most inspirational experience of my life. I am deeply grateful. I want to share my favorite story with you. There were these two Polacks . . ."

"Excuse me, my son," the Pope interrupted, "but are you aware that I'm Polish?"

"Yes, your Holiness," the man continued. "But don't worry—I'll go slow."

What's a Polish vibrator?

A mop handle and six relatives shaking the bed.

What do you get when you cross a Polack and a Puerto Rican?

A guy who spray paints graffiti on chain link fences.

Why aren't there many black skiers?

Because it's hard to ski with a pole in one hand and a radio in the other.

An Arab sheik visiting New York fell madly in love with the wife of an oil company executive. Not being shy, he approached the husband and said, "I must sleep with your wife. In return, I'll pay her weight in gold."

The executive hesitated a moment, then said, "Give me a few days."

"To think it over?" the sheik asked.

"Hell, no. To fatten her up."

What will it take to bring the Beatles back together?

Three more bullets.

Why can't you go to the bathroom at a Beatles concert?

There's no John.

What's yellow and sleeps alone?

Yoko Ono.

The sheriff arrived at the scene of the horrible accident just as one of his deputies climbed off a bulldozer. "What's happening?" the sheriff asked.

"Bus full of migrant workers went off the road and turned over. I just finished burying them."

"Sounds awful," the sheriff said. "Must have been messy. Were all of them dead?"

The deputy nodded. "Yep. Course, some of them said they weren't—but you know how those Mexicans lie."

A tramp was wandering down an alley when he came upon a rusty old lamp. Thinking he might be able to pawn it for a couple of bucks, he picked it up and began to rub it clean. To his surprise, the lamp gave forth a cloud of smoke and a genie appeared. The genie offered him three wishes.

The tramp thought, then said, "I want a million dollars."

The genie waved his hand, and a huge stack of bills appeared in a cloud of smoke.

The tramp said, "I want a Rolls Royce."

Another cloud of smoke, and a gleaming automobile, complete with liveried chauffeur, appeared.

"Wow!" the tramp said. He thought about his third wish for a minute. Then with a smile he said, "I want a dick that can touch the ground."

The genie cut his legs off.

Why are clams like women?

When the red tide comes in, you don't eat them.

A woman was out walking her dog when a man came up to admire the animal. "What's your dog's name?" he asked.

"Herpes," the woman replied.

"Herpes? That's weird. Why do you call him that?"

"Because he won't heel," the woman replied.

A farmer's stock wasn't breeding enough to suit him, so he went out and bought a sack of Spanish fly. When he was taking it out to the barn to mix it with the feed, he tripped on a rake and dropped the whole sack down the well. That evening he called the vet, complaining, "My stock's gone wild. The goat's chasing the sow; the cock's chasing the ducks, and the bull is after a young mare."

The doctor said, "Well, you've got to do something. Get outside and throw some cold water on them."

The farmer said, "I can't. My wife is humping the pump handle."

A young Army recruit decided to end his virginity by visiting a cathouse. He went off to a room with a hooker, who offered him one of three styles of sex—missionary style, doggie style, or 69. The boy didn't have any idea what she was talking about, but he said 69 sounded fine.

After some fumbling, the boy got into position and they were going at it when the hooker let out a stinky fart. The recruit didn't say anything, just continued on until the girl let pop another fart in his face. Shortly afterward, she asked the boy how he liked it.

"Just fine," the boy said. "But I don't think I can take 67 more of those stinkers."

A straight "F" student, Jimmy had been expelled from a half a dozen schools for fighting, destroying property, swearing at teachers, etc. At his rope's end, his father finally went to the priest, who suggested that Jimmy be enrolled in a Catholic school.

The father was skeptical, but he finally agreed. To his surprise, after a month, Jimmy brought home a report card with straight A's. Bewildered, his father asked Jimmy what happened.

"Well," Jimmy said, "the first day I sat down and looked up at the wall. I saw this kid nailed to a cross. So I figured right away this was the wrong place to fuck around."

A woman woke up in the hospital after an operation to find her doctor standing over her. The doctor said, "I've got some good news and some bad news for you."

"Give me the bad news first," the woman said.

"Well," the doctor said, "I'm afraid we found tumors in both breasts and we had to amputate both of them."

"My God!" the woman shrieked. "What could possibly be the good news?"

"The transvestite in the next bed wants to buy all of your old bras."

A young woman called her doctor and said in a deep voice, "Doc, I think you've given me too many hormone injections."

The physician replied, "Don't let that worry you, miss. That deep voice is a normal reaction. It will disappear in a few weeks."

"But I've also sprouted hair between my breasts," the woman complained.

"That is unusual," the doctor said. "How far down does it go?"

"All the way to my testicles," the woman replied.

How do women in Hollywood avoid pregnancy?

Easy. They just spit the sperm out the window.

A homosexual couple were spending a quiet evening at home when one turned and called out, "Bruce, has the paperboy come yet?"

"No, honey," Bruce replied, "but he's breathing very hard."

A girl was complaining to her friend that her boyfriend wouldn't fuck her—all he wanted to do was eat her out.

"If you want to stop that," her friend said, "I've got an idea. Just rub garlic on your pussy before you go to bed."

A few days later, her friend called, grumpier than usual. "Didn't it work?" she was asked.

"No," the girl said. "He just went to the refrigerator and came back with lettuce and olive oil."

A man went to the doctor to get his penis examined. The doctor, after examining the bruised, hugely swollen organ, asked him what happened.

"Well," the man said, "my next-door neighbor is this really well-built blonde. I started peeking into her kitchen. Every night she'd come in, take a hot dog from the refrigerator, stick it in the mail slot in the door, and ram herself against it, having a ball."

"So what?" the doctor said.

"Then I got this idea. One night when she turned around, I pulled the hot dog out and stuck my cock through the slot. Everything was going great until the front doorbell rang."

"What happened?"

"She panicked," the patient said. "She started kicking the hot dog."

Every time a very gay young guy walked by the corner hangout, the gang always hooted, "Hi, there, cunt."

The fag always smiled, nodded his head, and continued on. One day, however, when the punks called out, "Hi, there, cunt," the homosexual glared and said, "Don't ever call me cunt again."

"Why not?" one gang member asked.

"Because," the indignant fag said, "the other day, I saw one."

It was the first Christmas, and the Three Wise Men were walking into the stable. They nearly reached the manger when one stepped in a big pile of cow shit.

Looking down at his ruined gold slippers, the Wise Man spat, "Jesus Christ!"

Mary looked up from her infant and said to her husband, "Hey, Joseph. That's a much better name than Irving."

An old man went to his doctor to complain of toilet problems.

"Do you urinate all right?" the doctor asked.

"Every morning at seven," the old man said.

"Do you have bowel movements?"

"Every morning at eight," the old man replied.

"Well, you're regular," the doctor said. "What's your problem?"

"My problem is, I don't wake up until nine."

After twenty-seven years of marriage, the wife told her husband that she wanted him to eat her pussy, that it was a thrilling experience. Her husband was reluctant, but finally she talked him into it.

He got to work. He found the taste was okay, but the smell was overwhelming. But he stuck to it. Finally, his wife orgasmed and, at the same time, let go with a tremendous fart.

"Thank God!" the husband sighed. "A breath of fresh air!"

A man was studying the menu at a diner. He asked the waiter, "What's the difference between the blue-plate special and the white-plate special?"

"The white-plate special is a dollar more," the waiter said.

"Is the food better?" the man asked.

"No," the waiter replied. "But we wash the plate."